QuickArt

Crayon Projects

BY ROBIN BERNARD

SCHOLASTIC
PROFESSIONAL BOOKS

NEW YORK • TORONTO • LONDON • AUCKLAND • SYDNEY
MEXICO CITY • NEW DELHI • HONG KONG

For Ellen Winograd,

an extraordinary teacher,

and, as always, for JL.

Cover design by Norma Ortiz
Interior design by Kathy Massaro
Interior illustrations by Robin Bernard except pages 10, 15, 24, 41–42, 44, 49, 55, 61–62,
and the leaf and face on page 12, by James Graham Hale

ISBN 0-590-98339-3

Contents

Introduction

It only takes some crayons and a few other basic materials to lead your students on an exciting artistic journey. Children are natural artists: They appreciate beauty, they love to create, they have extraordinary imaginations, and they are energized by hands-on activities. Art offers children infinite possibilities without the pressure of "right or wrong" answers. Through the creative process, children gain confidence in their decision-making ability as well as their artistic ability.

In many schools, there is only one art teacher. Depending on the size of the school, this often does not allow children sufficient time in the art room. This book is designed for teachers who would like to offer their students more artistic opportunities in their own classrooms. The activities are easy to set up, require only basic art supplies, and the end results are dazzling!

paintings, but there are other less expensive options. Look for posters at bookstores, print shops, and second-hand stores. You can also cover a bulletin board with interesting, colorful images cut from magazines. Clip articles about art from newspapers or magazines and hang them on a board entitled "Art Makes the Headlines." And, of course, your students' masterpieces should always be on display!

Keeping art supplies neat and organized is important in making the process of creating art more appealing. This should be everyone's responsibility, not just the teacher's! Show the students where everything is kept and how to clean up when they are done. After looking through the activities to see what basic materials are needed, collect storage containers such as shoe boxes or large coffee cans. Label the containers so students can find materials easily and can clean up quickly.

Getting Started

Creating an art-filled atmosphere in your classroom will inspire students to be creative. First, gather some books about artists and art techniques and place them in a comfortable area for students to explore and enjoy on their own. (Libraries often carry wonderful collections of art books. There are specific suggestions on page 64.) Display a particular book or art poster prominently each week along with an inviting question for students to answer, such as, "How would you describe Mona Lisa's mood?" or "How do Picasso's blue paintings make you feel?" You can leave a stack of index cards for students to write their responses on, or you can raise the question during class discussion.

Find some colorful art posters and display them around the room or in a designated art area. Museum shops and catalogs offer posters of famous

How to Use This Book

There is no right or wrong way to use this book. These fun and easy activities will fuel your students' creativity while developing their fundamental artistic skills. Basic concepts are reinforced throughout the book, from learning to see shapes to exploring the endless possibilities of color and patterns.

Each chapter focuses on one concept and builds upon ideas in previous chapters. However, you don't need to follow the order of the book; the activities are simple enough to stand on their own. Use the ones that are appropriate for your class and adapt them as you see fit. You may find that some work well with other parts of your curriculum. For example, the "All About Us" Quilt might complement a social studies topic, while Cool Camouflage would be appropriate in conjunction with a unit on insects.

Each lesson is organized into sections for easy reference:

MATERIALS A short list of needed supplies

WHAT TO DO Step-by-step project instructions

Some activities include follow-up ideas:

KEEP GOING... Suggestions for a quick extension of the activity or topics for a closing discussion

BONUS ACTIVITY A related project that goes one step further

Chapter Introductions

Chapter 1 ● Lines and Shapes

When youngsters draw often, they become comfortable with their crayons quickly. But what takes more time and practice and concentration is learning to see—that is, learning to analyze and evaluate lines, shapes, and the spaces around shapes. This ability will give students greater control of their artwork and greater appreciation for art in general. The activities in this chapter are designed to help young artists sharpen their "seeing" skills as well as their drawing skills.

Chapter 2 ● Patterns

Patterns are everywhere—from the flowers on wallpaper to the stripes on a zebra! Working with patterns will help your students recognize and use designs in innovative and beautiful ways. They will enjoy discovering the effects of patterns in their own work as well as in the outside world.

Chapter 3 ● Color

Color often determines the atmosphere of a painting or drawing, and it can even affect the mood of the viewer. In these activities, students use color not as decoration but as its own powerful element. Famous paintings and scenes from nature can provide great inspiration for using color in stunning ways!

Chapter 4 ● Texture

Using different mediums and tools (even your own fingers!) creates terrific textures. Students will have fun giving their artwork more dimension with bumps, zigzags, crisscrosses, and other textures rubbed from everyday objects.

Chapter 5 ● Viewpoint and Size

Finding a new viewpoint is a quick way to make a piece of art more interesting. Looking at ordinary objects from a new angle—from below or above, from close-up or far away—suddenly makes them special. Using a more dramatic scale also adds excitement to a project. Students will enjoy enlarging drawings using a technique with grids that is so easy it seems like magic!

Chapter 6 ● Creative Activities

These playful activities draw upon all the skills from previous chapters. They are designed to spark children's imagination and help them generate their own creative ideas. As your students work on these projects, encourage them to use their knowledge of line, color, texture, and so on to develop their own unique styles.

Chapter 7 ● A Celebration of Art

"Art is a language," the saying goes, "and you don't learn a language to talk to yourself!" Art is meant to be shared and appreciated. Display your students' artwork in your classroom, in the halls, or even at a gala student exhibition! Nothing is quite so encouraging to artists of any age as taking part in an art show. This chapter provides ideas for framing student artwork and planning an exhibition.

Engage your students in constant dialogue about art—their own, their classmates', or art found in books and magazines. Some libraries offer slides of drawings and paintings, but a class trip to an art museum would be the best inspiration of all.

Silly Circles

Turn circles into fun characters and objects.

A circle is a familiar shape—and one that lends itself to creating all kinds of creatures and objects. In this activity, children transform circles into their own imaginative creations. To start, ask children what things they can think of that are round. The youngest students may need some help, so you might ask them leading questions, such as: *What tells time? What can you make out of snow? What foods are round? What round things are in the sky? What round things do you use to play games or sports?*

Materials

@ reproducible sheet (page 7)
@ crayons
@ extra paper

What to Do

1 Distribute copies of page 7.

2 Invite students to draw on the circles to make characters or objects.

3 If there aren't enough circles to accommodate all of their ideas, have children make their own circles (they don't need to be perfect!) on another piece of paper.

4 To display the finished pieces, cut out one or more large circles from colored craft paper. Hang students' work on the circles and entitle the display "Circular Sensations."

Keep Going...

Have children tally the number of balloons, snowmen, and so on in their drawings. Help them chart the results on a colorful bar graph.

Bonus Activity

Draw circles of different sizes on a piece of paper and photocopy it on plain or colored paper. Give each student one or two of the photocopied sheets and ask them to cut out the circles. Next, have them arrange the circles into interesting formations and glue them on paper of a different color. Then invite students to draw on their circles to create all kinds of objects or creatures—real or imaginary. This can also be repeated with other shapes or a variety of shapes.

Name _____ Date _____

Silly Circles

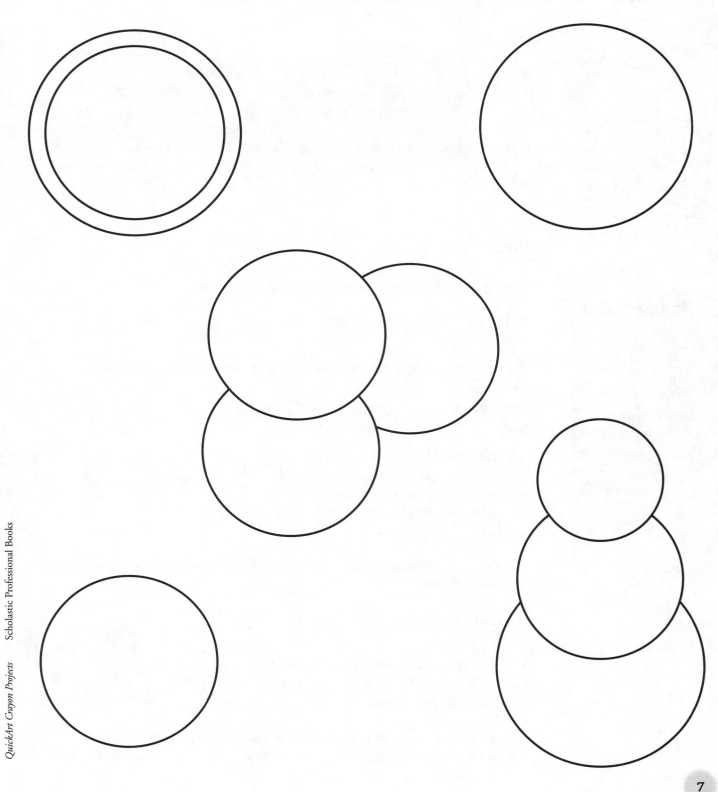

Squiggles & Squaggles

Transform squiggly lines and shapes into zany creatures.

This fun, ten-minute activity will help children see how simple lines and squiggles can be transformed into funny animals or people—all they have to do is add eyes, ears, hair, or even scales and feathers. Your students will have to look closely at the squiggly lines to figure out how to transform them (a good way to develop their "seeing" skills).

Materials

@ reproducible sheet (page 9)

@ crayons, colored pencils, or markers

@ extra paper

What to Do

First, demonstrate how to turn the squiggles into people.

1 Draw a bold squiggle on the board.

2 Find the section that protrudes the most and turn it into a nose.

3 Next draw the eye, mouth, hair, and other features.

4 Add details like glasses, earrings, a mustache, and so on. Encourage students to add humor to their drawings by adding unusual touches, like a mohawk or a silly hat.

Then show how the amoeba-shaped "squaggles" can be made into whimsical imaginary critters.

1 Draw a bold squaggle on the board.

2 Add eyes, funny ears, a nose or snout, whiskers, tusks, fur, feathers, scales, claws, or even polka dots!

3 Distribute copies of page 9 and invite students to transform the squiggles and squaggles into fun creatures, as you have demonstrated.

Squiggles & Squaggles

Double Doodles

Tape two markers together to make super swirling abstracts!

Doodling is a great way to introduce children to abstract designs, and double doodling is twice as much fun! Begin by demonstrating the technique on a large sheet of newsprint so that everyone can see. Tape two colored markers together and draw swirling loops and angles. Swirls and figure eights produce dramatic "ribbons." Then color in a section to show students how this emphasizes both the shapes and the spaces between the shapes, called negative space.

What to Do

Materials

- crayons
- markers
- tape
- paper

1 Help students tape their markers together, making sure that both points touch a flat surface when held perpendicularly.

2 Allow children practice time to grow accustomed to holding their twin markers perpendicular to the paper.

3 Suggest that they move their arms as they draw—not just their wrists—and encourage them to make loops and angles. Only six or seven movements will do the trick; too many lines on the paper will muddle the design.

4 Once the designs are drawn, students can use crayons to color all the "ribbons" as well as the spaces between them.

Teacher's Note

These colorful designs look great as decorative covers for student writing. You might also have students "double doodle" on large pieces of colored paper, then fold them in half for beautiful folders in which to store artwork.

Sensational Symmetry

Complete the symmetry of four drawings.

Symmetry is a fascinating concept, and one that is found everywhere—in nature, in math, and also in art! This quick exercise is a great way to introduce the concept to young artists and to encourage them to look for symmetry all around them. Explain to your students that *symmetrical* means having similar parts on both halves. Invite the class to brainstorm a list of symmetrical things, and write their ideas on the board.

◎ What symmetrical features do people have? (Eyes, ears, hands, feet, and so on)

◎ What do we wear that's symmetrical? (Sweaters, socks, glasses, earrings, and so on)

◎ What things in nature are symmetrical? (Certain leaves, flowers, shells, butterflies, beetles, crabs, and so on)

What to Do

1 Distribute a copy of page 12 to each student.

2 Explain that each of the four sections has half of a drawing. All the objects are symmetrical, so the missing parts will be mirror images of the ones they see. You may want to cut apart the pictures on page 12 and hold them against a mirror to show the "magic" of symmetry.

3 Ask students to look at the drawings carefully and then complete the symmetry.

4 When they are finished, they can color the drawings with crayons.

Keep Going...

Challenge students to think of other symmetrical things and draw only half of them (following the examples in the exercise). Then have them switch papers with a partner and complete each other's drawings symmetrically.

Materials
◎ reproducible sheet (page 12)
◎ pencils
◎ crayons

Name _____ Date _____

Sensational Symmetry

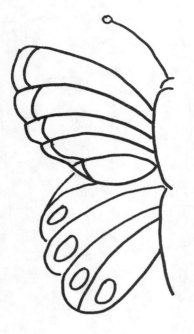

QuickArt Crayon Projects   Scholastic Professional Books

Upside-Down Art

Copy an upside-down picture for a realistic effect.

Even professional illustrators feel a degree of tension when drawing realistically, so it's no wonder that beginners become frustrated. And it's exactly that concern with realism that gets in the way. Children tend to look at an object instead of the shape or shapes that form the object. Here's a fun experiment that seems silly, but it will actually teach children a crucial drawing maxim: SHAPE is the secret! When your students are copying an upside-down model picture, they won't be hampered by realistic content. Instead, they will be able to concentrate on lines, shapes, and the spaces between shapes, and they will be pleasantly surprised by the results!

What to Do

1 Give each child a copy of page 14. Pass out the pictures so they are facing upside down. Ask students to keep the pages facing that way.

2 Have students place the blank sheet on top of the reproducible and trace the box. Then have them place the sheets side by side.

3 Tell students to forget all about what's in the picture! Encourage them to draw what they see, concentrating on lines, shapes, and spaces between shapes.

4 When students are finished, have them turn the model drawing right side up and compare it to their drawings. They can then color their drawings with crayons.

5 Discuss the results as a group. Were children surprised by their drawings? What did they find out about this method? Was it harder or easier than drawing the regular way?

Materials
- reproducible sheet (page 14)
- pencils
- paper
- crayons

Bonus Activity

Have students bring in a picture of a favorite animal or person to draw using the same upside-down procedure. Then display the drawings next to the original pictures with the title "Utterly Upside Down." Include a brief explanation of the upside-down method.

Upside-Down Art

QuickArt Crayon Projects   Scholastic Professional Books

Shadow Play

Use shadows as models to create bold silhouettes.

Here's a neat variation on drawing objects or models—draw their shadows instead! By focusing on a clear shadow, children can concentrate on the shape of an object without getting bogged down by details. Once they have drawn the perimeter, they can fill in both the shape and the background with solid colors or patterns. The finished pieces will be striking in their bold contrast. Display them in the hall with a challenge for viewers to guess the objects that projected these shadows. You can leave a blank index card by each drawing for viewers to write down their guesses and then circle the correct answers.

What to Do

First, make the shadow box:

1 Cut off (or fold back) the front and back flaps of a cardboard carton.

2 Tape tissue paper to the front opening, keeping it as taut as you can.

3 Place an object with a clearly defined shape behind the tissue paper. (A leafy plant or a vase of flowers works well.)

4 Lower the window shades and turn off the overhead lights so the room is dim but not dark. Use a flashlight behind the object to throw it into silhouette.

Materials

Shadow Box

◎ cardboard carton
◎ scissors
◎ tape
◎ tissue paper
◎ large flashlight
◎ model objects

Drawing Materials

◎ pencils
◎ crayons, markers, or acrylic paint
◎ paper

15

Teacher's Note

If your class is large, it would be best to set up two shadow boxes so that everyone has a good view.

Tell your students to:

1 Start by drawing just the outline of what they see in pencil.

2 Try to fill at least two-thirds of the paper with their drawing.

3 When their outline is complete, fill it with a solid color or even a simple pattern. Students can do this with either crayons, markers, or paint. Then have them color the background. If they want to use a pattern, they should use it for either the object or the background, not both. (This way their objects will not get lost in the patterns.)

Suggestions for model objects: toy trucks, trains, dolls, or stuffed animals; boots or sneakers; figurines or sculptures; interesting lamps or vases; opaque bottles and glasses; a guitar, trumpet, or another instrument with curves

Classmate Cameos

Trace profiles for a sensational Who's Who game.

In this activity, everyone's a model—and everyone's an artist! By casting the model's shadow onto newsprint on the wall, students can trace each other's silhouetted profile realistically. It's fun, it's easy, and the results look very professional!

What to Do

1 Tape a sheet of newsprint to the wall.

2 Have the student model stand sideways with one shoulder touching the wall and with his or her face turned toward the artist's "drawing" hand. (This avoids the artist's having to reach across the model's face to draw.)

3 Dim the room and position a lamp or flashlight to shine at the model. This will project the model's silhouette onto the newsprint. Then the artist can simply trace in pencil the outlined profile directly onto the paper.

4 When all the silhouette outlines have been drawn, students can use black crayons or markers to fill them in.

5 Have them sign their drawings on the front and put the name of their model on the back.

Keep Going...

Display the profiles on a bulletin board entitled "Do you recognize these classmate cameos?" Engage students in a guessing game to figure out who's who.

Materials
- large sheets of newsprint
- large flashlights or gooseneck lamps
- tape
- pencils
- black crayons or markers

Teacher's Note

Set up several stations in your room where students can take turns working on this activity in pairs. Students can trade their finished drawings with each other so that they can take home silhouettes of themselves.

"All About Us" Quilt

Assemble a class quilt with a square about each student.

Making a classroom quilt is a great way to start the year and get to know your class. Students work together in this cooperative project and contribute their own artistic styles to the finished product. Before you begin, show your students samples of quilting patterns from a book and lead a short discussion. When was quilting a popular activity? What purposes do they think it served? If they do not already know the social aspects of quilting, the follow-up questions at the end will help.

Materials

◎ crayons and markers
◎ squares of white paper
◎ squares of colored paper
◎ tape

Teacher's Note

Cut 2 inches off the tops of 8 1/2- x 11-inch paper to make 8 1/2- x 8 1/2-inch squares.

What to Do

1 Divide the class into small groups of four or five students. Ask each group to sit in a circle as they design their squares. (This will make their experience similar to a traditional quilting group.)

2 Distribute markers and crayons to each group and give each student a white paper square.

3 Invite students to design a square that reflects their individual interests and personality. Before they begin drawing, ask them to consider what they enjoy and what is important to them. Remind them to include their name somewhere on their square. For best results, have students color in a border around their square so that it will have definition when the quilt is assembled.

4 When everyone has finished, ask the class to decide cooperatively upon a pattern for the quilt. You can suggest some possibilities, such as girl-boy or girl-girl-boy-boy. They might also arrange the squares in a pattern according to the objects depicted or the colors of the borders. Use the colored paper to make a bolder pattern. Students can then tape the squares together to form the quilt.

Teacher's Note

Use tape on the back of the squares so that it does not show.

Keep Going...

◎ After they have assembled the quilt, ask how the groups worked together. Did they work quietly or did they talk? Did they talk about other topics besides their quilt? Do they think that this is typical of a group working on a quilt?

◎ You can use the quilt as a way for students to introduce themselves to the class. Ask students to explain how their squares tell something about themselves. Hang the quilt in the hall or in the classroom for everyone to enjoy!

Pattern Pictures

Trace animal template patterns for super springtime designs.

Celebrate spring with colorful pattern pictures that are a snap to create! Students make their own templates by simply pasting the patterns onto oaktag and cutting them out. Then they trace the templates and color them in for beautiful springtime creations! This activity will allow students to focus on the outlines of shapes and experiment with making shapes work together.

Materials

- reproducible sheet (page 22)
- oaktag
- paste
- scissors
- pencils
- white or pastel-colored paper
- crayons or markers

What to Do

First, have students follow these steps to make their own templates:

1 Paste one of the patterns on page 22 onto oaktag.

2 Cut the pattern out along the dark line.

Next, invite them to make a pattern picture. You may want to demonstrate these steps first:

1 Use a pencil to trace the template on drawing paper. Start by tracing two or three "close" ones near the bottom of the page.

2 As you trace the ones farther up on the page, let the ones in front overlap the ones in back. To do this, lift your pencil anytime it would pass through the outline of the shape in front of it. This will make the ones in the back look farther away.

Teacher's Note

Remind kids that it's okay to goof—that's why there are erasers.

3 Have children color their pattern pictures. They can add stripes, spots, eyes, antennae, or anything else they think would be eye-catching. They can also use glitter to make the fish look like they are shimmering in water.

Keep Going...

Have some math fun with the finished patterns. For instance, you might ask, "If a fisherman caught all of Student A's fish and all of Student B's fish, how many would he have?" Or have students total all the butterflies and then ask them to deduct x number of them to start a butterfly garden. How many would be left?

Invite children to draw their own templates—other animals or just fun designs—and then make pattern pictures with them.

Pattern
Pictures

QuickArt Crayon Projects   Scholastic Professional Books

Terrific Tessellations!

Create beautiful tessellations with ready-made templates.

In Latin, the word *tessella* means "small stone." A collection of small stones that have been assembled into a pattern is a *tessellation*, or what we generally call a mosaic. What's great fun about using tessellations is that they fit together like puzzle pieces! You can either have students use the ready-made templates or, if you have more advanced students, you can challenge them to design their own. Either way, your students will enjoy creating tessellations. Before you get started, show your students some of M. C. Escher's awe-inspiring tessellations.

What to Do

First, have each student prepare a ready-made template:

1 Distribute a copy of page 25 to each student.

2 Ask students to choose one shape and cut it out.

3 Then have students trace their shape onto an index card or a piece of oaktag and cut it out.

Next, pass out pencils and paper and have students follow these steps to make their tessellation:

1 Using a sharpened pencil, trace the template anywhere on the paper.

2 Next, without turning or flipping the template, slide it in any direction until it "fits" into the first shape, like two puzzle pieces.

3 Keep sliding and tracing until the row is finished. Then slide the template over to start another row, making sure that the template fits onto the shapes in the first row. Continue until the page is full.

Materials
- reproducible sheet (page 25)
- index cards or oaktag
- pencils
- scissors
- crayons
- paper

4 Color the tessellations using solid colors, stripes, polka dots, or any other patterns.

Bonus Activity

Challenge students to create their own templates by following these steps. They will need a pencil, tape, and either a piece of oaktag or an index card.

1 Draw a very simple half-shape on one side of the oaktag (for example, half of a diamond, circle, or triangle) and cut it out.

2 Slide the cut piece to the opposite side of the oaktag square and tape it there.

3 Repeat the first two steps, cutting the piece from one side of the oaktag square and taping it to the other side of the square.

4 Using the template, follow steps 1–4 above to make a cool new tessellation!

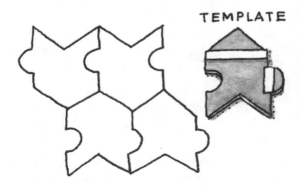

TEMPLATE

Terrific Tessellations!

Concerto for Crayons

Draw musically inspired designs.

Open a discussion by asking why so many artists and illustrators like to listen to music while they work. Does it set a mood? Ask your students how different kinds of music make them feel. How does music in a scary movie make them feel? What about the music in a Western or in a cartoon?

Explain to your students that they will be drawing freely while listening to music, trying to capture the mood of the music in their picture. Encourage them to think about how color, line, shape, and texture all contribute to the "mood" of a drawing or painting. For example, flowing lines and light colors could depict soft, melodious music while jagged lines and bright colors could represent harsh-sounding music.

Materials

- reproducible sheet (page 27)
- crayons or colored pencils
- recorded music
- tape player or CD player

What to Do

1 Distribute a copy of page 27 to each student.

2 Explain that you're going to play short passages from four different kinds of music.

3 Tell them to draw something in each quadrant that the musical excerpt brings to mind. Remind them that their drawings need not be realistic. Making abstract designs with colors and shapes works best! (Have students use the same quadrant for each musical piece so that they can compare their drawings later.)

4 When students have finished, hang up their pictures for discussion. Were similar images or colors evoked by the same music? Why do they suppose that happened? Invite students to give each of their drawings titles.

Teacher's Note

The results will be much more interesting if the four musical selections are distinctly different and preferably without lyrics. Only play about 60–90 seconds of each selection. (Students will keep drawing as long as the music is on; if it goes on too long, they'll muddy their designs.)

Suggestions for music: Sousa march, African drum music, Chopin etude, jazz, bagpipes, blues, The Beach Boys, The Beatles, opera, synthesized music

Concerto for Crayons

Stained Glass Designs

Design decorative and colorful paper windows.

Stained glass is a striking art form—full of intense colors—that is traditionally used for windows, lamps, and even jewelry. Here's an easy way for children to create pictures that resemble stained glass. Show students examples of stained glass from books or magazines and note the shapes, lines, color, and dramatic contrast.

Materials

- black tempera paint
- glue
- squeeze bottle with pointed cap
- paper
- crayons
- cooking oil
- brushes

What to Do

1 In a squeeze bottle, mix equal parts of black tempera paint and school glue. Shake well to distribute the color evenly. (A wooden skewer or the wooden end of a long paintbrush can also be used to stir the mixture.)

2 Have students squirt (or paint) thin lines of the mixture on paper where they want the "lead" to appear. Before they begin, talk about the kind of shapes they might want to use: circles, rectangles, diamonds, shapes inside of other shapes, shapes of all different sizes, made-up shapes, patterns, borders, and so on.

3 Let the lines dry thoroughly.

4 Ask students to fill in the "glass" areas with crayons. Encourage them first to think about what colors they will use.

5 Have them brush a thin coat of oil over the colored sections and let dry.

Teacher's Note

These look fabulous mounted on black paper. Glue the stained glass in the center so that the black paper shows from behind like a frame. Hang these on the windows in your room or in the hallway for a festive display, and then send them home as holiday gifts!

Cool Camouflage

Hide cutout creepy crawlers in colorful garden settings.

This activity is an excellent addition to a science unit about the colors we see in nature. These colors are not only delightful to look at but also highly useful to certain animals. Nectar-sipping insects, birds, and bats, for instance, are attracted to flowers of specific colors; bright red insects and amphibians are safe from predators because their colors warn that they're poisonous; and hundreds of animals—from tiny bugs to Bengal tigers—benefit from having colors that keep them hidden in their habitats. Each student can research how color helps a particular animal. (Some examples are polar bears, tree frogs, toads, stick insects, praying mantises, cheetahs, Arctic foxes, and lions.)

What to Do

1 Distribute a copy of page 30 to each student.

2 Before coloring the insects, discuss which colors are realistic for a butterfly, a ladybug, and an inchworm. Then ask students to color the insects accordingly.

3 Explain that students will help the insects hide in the gardens. Ask them to spend a few minutes deciding which colors to use for the garden so that they can hide the insects.

4 Finally, have children cut out the insects and paste them onto the garden picture so that they are camouflaged.

Keep Going...

Have a bug hunt! Display the pictures with a challenge for viewers to find the creepy crawlers.

Bonus Activity

Have students cooperatively make a mural of a rain forest. (Use paint, markers, crayons, or all three on a large sheet of craft paper.) Then have each student create a paper critter to hide in the mural.

Materials

@ reproducible sheet (page 30)
@ crayons
@ scissors
@ paste

Name _____ Date _____

Cool Camouflage

QuickArt Crayon Projects   Scholastic Professional Books

Magical Appearance

Paint over a crayon drawing for a neat surprise!

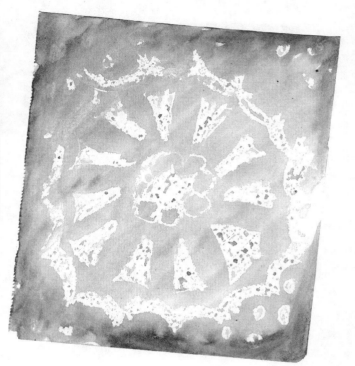

This activity will make kids feel like they are performing a magic trick! First kids draw on white paper using white crayon, so the drawing is "hidden." Then they use the technique of resist painting as they paint a layer of watercolor paint over their drawings. The paint will be resisted by the crayon wax, suddenly defining the previously camouflaged crayon drawing.

What to Do

1 Pass out a sheet of paper and a crayon to each student.

2 Invite students to draw a design. It can be a bit tricky to draw with a white crayon, but they can keep their drawings simple.

3 Next have them brush a wash of watercolor paint over their drawings. The paint will outline and give definition to the crayon drawing, making it appear as if by magic!

Teacher's Note

This is a fun activity to tie into holiday or seasonal celebrations. Try using green paint for St. Patrick's Day, red for Valentine's Day, orange for Halloween, and so on.

Materials

- ◎ white construction paper
- ◎ white crayons
- ◎ watercolor paints
- ◎ medium or wide brushes

Dynamic Duo

Use a trick with chalk and crayons to make one drawing turn into two!

Materials

- black or dark-colored crayons
- colored chalk
- paper (Cut 8 1/2- x 11-inch paper in half or in quarters.)
- pencils

What to Do

Have students follow these steps. You may want to demonstrate them first.

1 Use chalk to color the entire paper with geometric shapes, patterns, or other designs.

2 Tap the paper over a trashcan to remove excess dust. Do not spray a fixative.

3 Using a black or dark-colored crayon, completely color over the chalk.

4 Place a second piece of paper on top of the first. Draw a picture with pencil on the second sheet, pressing down firmly. Encourage students to fill in areas by using the side of the pencil. As they press the pencil down, the crayon is lifted from the first sheet and transferred to the underside of the second sheet.

5 When they are finished with their drawing, they can separate the papers and discover that they now have two drawings that are positive and negative images of each other. You can discuss this concept by pointing out where there is color in one drawing, there is no color in the other.

Teacher's Note

Display the two drawings next to each other to show the positive and negative images. Ask students how they think this process worked.

Color My Mood

Use crayon and watercolor to express a mood through color.

What does it mean to feel blue? Does the color blue really express the feeling? Ask students to think about this and consider if other colors have "moods." How do they feel when they look at bright yellow, deep red, or dark green? Show students paintings from an art book that are predominantly one color and ask them to describe the moods of the paintings. For example, you could look at several paintings from Picasso's blue period. How do they think the artist felt when he was painting these blue paintings? How do they think he wanted the viewers to feel?

What to Do

1 To start, ask students to choose a mood that they are going to represent using color. It can be the mood they are feeling or any mood that they think would make an interesting subject.

2 Pass out paper and crayons.

3 Invite students to think about the mood that they are going to depict and choose some colors to start with. They can use several different colors or they can use several shades of the same color.

4 Have students draw freely to express their moods, leaving some of the paper uncolored. They can draw realistically or they can express the mood through patterns, shapes, and designs.

5 When they are finished with their drawings, pass out watercolor paints, medium or wide brushes, and containers of water.

6 Ask students to cover the entire drawing with a wash of watercolor. They can use one or more colors. The areas that are colored will resist the paint while the uncolored areas will absorb it, creating an interesting effect.

Materials
- paper
- crayons
- watercolor paints
- brushes
- containers of water

Teacher's Note

When the paintings are dry, display them and ask other students to guess what moods they represent.

Crayon Batik

Create a textured drawing using crayon as wax resist.

Batik is an Indonesian method of handprinting textiles in which parts of the fabric are covered in wax to resist the dye. In this version, students create a textured picture using a similar technique with crayon wax.

Materials

- heavy brown wrapping paper cut into 8 1/2- x 11-inch pieces
- crayons
- pencils
- watercolor paints
- medium to wide brushes

Teacher's Note

Complement your students' batik drawings by mounting them on dark paper.

What to Do

1 Set up one or two buckets filled with water, or fill a sink with water if one is available.

Have students follow these steps to create their batik drawings. You may want to demonstrate each step first.

1 To start, sketch a drawing in pencil on the wrapping paper. You can set up a few objects for the students to draw, or you can take them outside to draw scenery.

2 Use crayon to add color to the drawings, leaving some sections of the paper uncolored.

3 Place the drawing in water, allowing the paper to absorb water.

4 Remove the paper and crumple it into a ball.

5 Uncrumple the paper and lay it flat.

6 Use a cloth or paper towel to absorb extra water. Blot rather than rub the water off.

7 Using a wide brush, apply a wash of watercolor over the entire drawing. The colored sections will resist the paint and the folds in the paper will create an appealing pattern.

8 Allow the drawing to dry thoroughly.

Funny Fingerprints

Decorate your fingerprints to make cute critters.

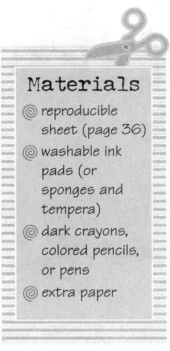

Is there a parent or teacher who hasn't occasionally wondered how one small child can manage to leave a zillion fingerprints on a freshly painted wall or otherwise sparkling window? Kids love to use textures—and they love to use their hands. Here's a great way for them to do both, and they'll also stretch their imaginations as they figure out how to turn their fingerprints into adorable little creatures.

What to Do

1 Distribute ink pads and copies of page 36. (Four children can share one ink pad. You can make your own ink pads by wetting sponges with a solution of tempera paint thinned with water.)

2 Invite the kids to make fingerprints on each row of the reproducible page. Remind them to leave some room between prints.

3 When the prints are thoroughly dry, distribute crayons, colored pencils, or pens for students to add whiskers, wings, eyes, arms, legs, antennae, and so on.

4 Encourage them to make up their own creatures rather than copy the model provided. Ask them to create the funniest animals they can. Whose insect has the most legs? Whose bird has the fanciest tail feathers? Have students come up with zany names for their creatures, such as "Fanny Fang Face" or "Tweety Long Legs."

Keep Going ...

Give students extra paper so that they can make additional fingerprint creations or experiment with clusters of prints (a great way to make flowers!).

Materials

- reproducible sheet (page 36)
- washable ink pads (or sponges and tempera)
- dark crayons, colored pencils, or pens
- extra paper

Bonus Activity

The fingerprint characters are quick to do and easy to replicate, so they are perfect for comic strips. Have students choose their favorite critter or two to use in their own original comic strip.

Name _____ Date _____

Funny Fingerprints

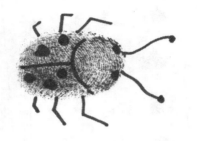

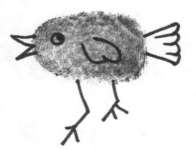

QuickArt Crayon Projects   Scholastic Professional Books

Reptile Rubbings

Explore new textures to create scaly reptiles.

Ask children to describe what texture means to them. Lead them to the consensus that it's the way something feels to the touch. Ask them to describe what these things feel like:

- popcorn
- hairbrush
- marbles

- sand
- towel
- feather

- rabbit
- thorns
- spaghetti

Textures can make a drawing look really exciting! Challenge your students to find textured surfaces that would make good rubbings. What terrific textures can they find right where they are? A zipper? A comb? What about the bottom of their sneakers?

What to Do

First, do a quick warm-up:

1 Pass out the texture grid on page 39.

2 Have students place their paper over a textured surface and rub it with a crayon. Ask them to rub a different texture in each box and then write what kind of surface produced that texture.

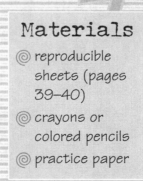

Materials

- reproducible sheets (pages 39–40)
- crayons or colored pencils
- practice paper

Teacher's note

Texture rubbings come out best when the side of a pencil or crayon is used. Encourage students to try using different colors to do their rubbings.

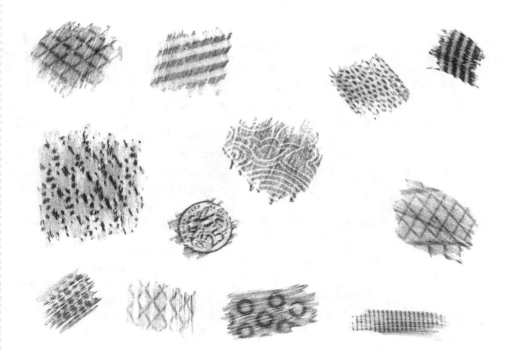

Next, have students choose their favorite texture to do their "reptile rubbing":

1 Distribute a copy of the lizard on page 40 to each student.

2 Ask students to choose a surface to do a texture rubbing on the lizard. The different textures and colors will make quite an interesting collection of reptiles! You can hang up each student's reptile rubbing beside his or her texture grid to show that these unusual textures come from quite ordinary objects.

Bonus Activity

Use crayons to rub a texture onto construction paper. Then brush a thin watercolor wash on top for a neat effect. These can be folded to make covers or folders, cut into shapes, or enjoyed as they are.

Reptile Rubbings

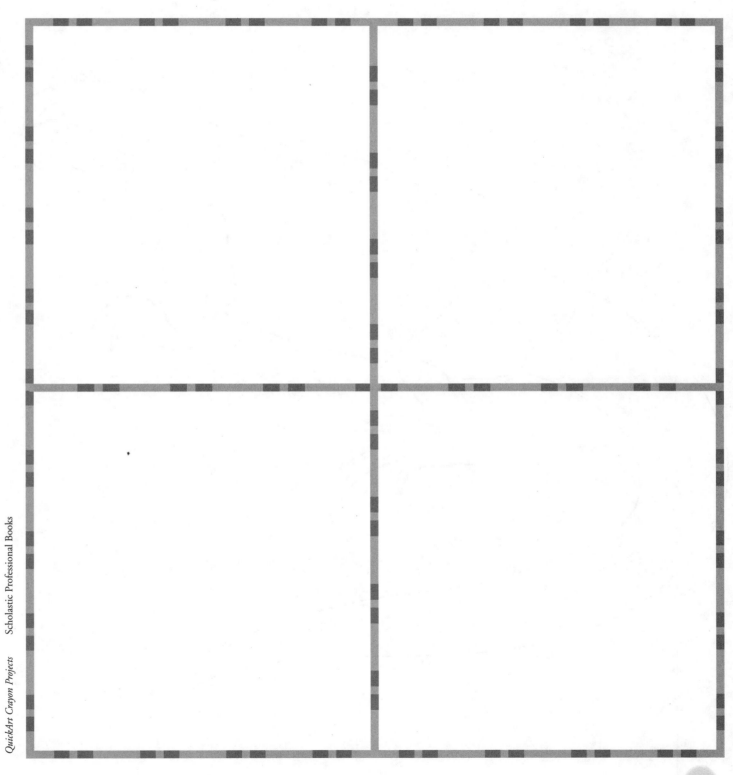

Reptile Rubbings

QuickArt Crayon Projects   Scholastic Professional Books

Monster Prints

Create a crayon rubbing of a cardboard cutout monster.

Students create monsters by arranging and then gluing pieces of cutout cardboard onto paper. To make monster prints, they use a rubbing technique called "frottage." They can then create several prints of different colors using the same monster template. Use the monsters to inspire creative writing or poetry. Ask students to name their monster and then write a story or poem with their creature as the main character.

What to Do

1 In advance, cut the cardboard into squares of various sizes. This will make it easier for the students to cut the cardboard into different shapes. If possible, provide both smooth and corrugated cardboard for varied textures.

2 Distribute cardboard and scissors.

3 Have students start by cutting out several different shapes. Encourage them to make shapes of varying sizes.

4 When students have cut out several shapes, invite them to "play" with the pieces to form a monster. They can cut and add more pieces as needed.

5 After students have decided what their monsters will look like, pass out paper and glue. Have them arrange and then glue the pieces onto the paper. Let the glue dry thoroughly.

Materials
- thin cardboard
- scissors
- glue or rubber cement
- paper
- crayons

You may want to demonstrate the next few steps for students.

1 Place a plain piece of paper on top of the monster and hold it firmly. (You may want to hold the paper in place with tape or a paper clip.)

2 Rub the side of an unwrapped crayon in one direction over the paper to make a "print" of the monster design.

3 Students can make several prints of their monster. They can use a different color for each print or they can use several colors in one print for a "rainbow monster."

4 Invite students to use markers and crayons to add facial features and other details to their monster prints. They can also glue on materials such as googly eyes and pipe cleaners for whiskers.

Teacher's Note

Mount the finished pieces on black paper and display your monsters for Halloween!

Mouse-Eye View

Draw an object close-up to create a mysterious image!

Ask students to imagine they are mice. How would things appear to them? Ordinary objects would look huge, and they'd only see the parts of things closest to them. Explain that many photographers challenge viewers to identify close-up pictures of familiar items. These close-ups are hard to figure out because we're too close to see the outer edge (or perimeter). By eliminating the perimeter, an object becomes a mystery! As an example, draw a rectangle on the board to represent a piece of paper, copy the figure below onto the "paper," and ask students to guess what it might be.

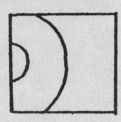

Could it be part of an eye? A piece of cereal? A doughnut? A toy wheel?

What to Do

First, guide students as they assemble their viewfinders.

1 Give each student a copy of page 45.

2 Use the bottom part of the reproducible for the viewfinder and set aside the top portion for drawing. Have them cut along the dashed lines to make two thick L-shapes.

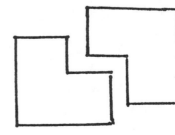
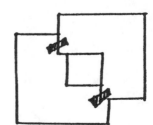

3 Tape the pieces together so that they form a small opening (about a 1-inch square).

Next, have students use the viewfinders to draw their mystery pictures.

1 Encourage students to explore the classroom through the frames and select an interesting image to draw in the small square. They should draw in the square on the right with the solid line at the top of their drawing. Tell them to get very close to the object they are drawing.

2 When children have finished their drawings, have them cut out both the drawing and the attached flap. (Remind them not to cut them apart.)

3 Ask them to fold the flap behind the drawing and write what their object is on the inside.

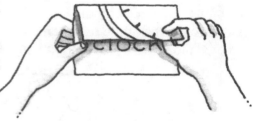

4 Display the drawings in your classroom or hallway. Challenge viewers to "solve the mystery drawings." Invite them to open up the pictures to reveal the answers underneath.

Mouse-Eye View

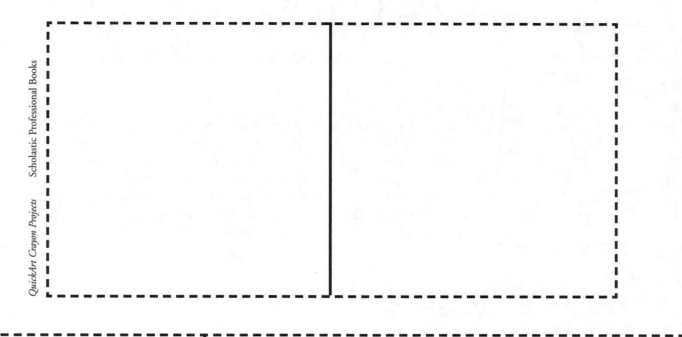

Getting Bigger

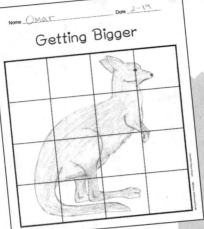

Use grids to enlarge animal drawings.

When young artists want to enlarge their drawings, they often have trouble scaling them up by eye. Using grids is an effective technique to make enlarging easier. Even professional artists use grids, especially if they are painting a mural. In this activity, kids will have fun helping animals "grow," and the finished product will amaze them! In addition, by concentrating on lines and shapes, they will also improve their "seeing" skills and drawing skills.

Materials

◎ reproducible sheets (pages 47–48)

◎ pencils and erasers

◎ crayons or colored pencils

What to Do

1 Distribute a copy of the animal page on page 47 and several extra copies of the grid on page 48 to each student.

2 Ask students to select an animal to copy. Point out that each square on the small grid corresponds to a square on the large grid.

3 Encourage children to study each square carefully. Then have them copy in pencil the shapes in each square of the small picture grid onto the corresponding square of the large grid. If the animal picture has an empty square, the artist needs to leave that particular square blank on the large grid and go on to the next one. Remind them to look carefully at the lines and shapes as they transfer them onto the larger grid. They can also look at the negative space in the small picture and compare it to their drawing. This will help them copy more accurately.

4 When they're satisfied with the enlargement, have children color their pictures with crayons or colored pencils.

5 Invite students to enlarge the remaining animals.

Keep Going...

Make an animal puzzle! After students have enlarged and colored their animals, have them glue their drawing to a piece of oaktag. Then they simply cut along the grid lines to make their own animal puzzle. Students can switch puzzles with a partner and try to put them back together.

Getting Bigger

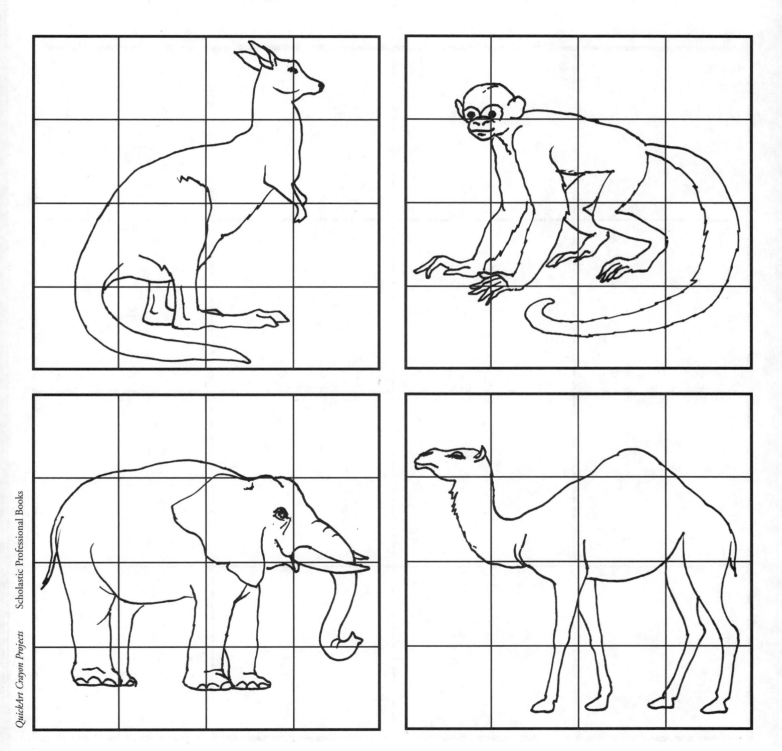

Getting Bigger

QuickArt Crayon Projects   Scholastic Professional Books

Mystery Mascot

Create a giant surprise with grids!

In this cooperative project, each class member enlarges one grid section of a dinosaur drawing. Students then assemble the pieces to create their own enormous class mascot! This is a great follow-up activity to Getting Bigger on page 46.

What to Do

Make two photocopies of page 51. Keep one hidden away as a reference page for yourself, and cut apart the other picture along the solid lines to make rectangular puzzle pieces. If there are less than 30 children in your class, give some students two puzzle pieces to copy along with extra paper. Later, when the puzzle pieces are assembled, the kids will discover that they've made a giant plateosaurus!

1 Give each child a puzzle piece and a sheet of blank paper.

2 Have students draw the puzzle piece's image so that it fills the 8 1/2- by 11-inch piece of paper. Before they begin, ask them to study the image carefully and stress that it's important for them to be as accurate as possible. As they work, circulate around the room to make sure they are looking carefully at lines and shapes.

Materials
- reproducible sheet (page 51)
- pencils
- erasers
- 30 sheets of 8 1/2- x 11-inch paper
- crayons

3 Clear a large space (at least four by six feet) on the floor to assemble the pieces. You may want to ask children to take turns putting their piece where they think it belongs. After each child has added a piece, students can take turns reassembling them as necessary. (You can use your hidden reference sheet to give them clues, if needed.)

4 Tape the pieces together and invite kids to measure the plateosaurus and compare its size with their own.

5 Now it's time to color the dinosaur. When children are finished, hang it on the classroom wall for everybody to enjoy.

6 Brainstorm a list of names for the new class mascot. Write their ideas on the board and have them vote for their favorite name.

Teacher's Note

You can use the dinosaur board as a fun message board. Make a title "_____ says…" (inserting the name of the dinosaur) and then attach messages written on talk balloons cut out of paper. The class mascot can remind students to return their library books on time or get their permission slips signed for a field trip.

Mystery Mascot

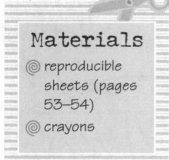

Just Imagine...

Jump-start creative drawing.

Even children who love creating art occasionally get stuck in the "what should I draw" dilemma. These easy activities will spark their imaginations and also help them generate their own creative ideas. Once students have finished the four drawings on the reproducible sheets, they can either refer to the list of imagination stretchers or they can come up with their own unique ideas.

What to Do

Distribute copies of pages 53–54 and ask your students to just imagine that …

1 while in Australia they caught a glimpse of a bird called the Rainbow Lorikeet, and they colored this picture to show their friends back home what it looked like.

2 they are decorating a window box and filling it with the brightest, prettiest flowers they can imagine.

3 archeologists discovered these bones in Montana and asked them to draw what they think the animal might have looked like.

4 the U.S. Postal Service asked them to design a brand-new stamp. The theme can be sports, flowers, space, animals, or another idea.

Imagination Stretchers!

List these and other ideas on a bulletin board in your art center to inspire your students when they don't know what to draw. Encourage them to contribute their own ideas to the list. Keep paper, pencils, markers, and crayons nearby so that everything will be ready to go!

◎ A new pattern for a zebra ◎ A new design for a one dollar bill ◎ A new logo for the "Save Our Planet" campaign ◎ A billboard for a Whale Watching Boat ◎ A silly kite ◎ Your own spaceship ◎ A deluxe tree house ◎ A map of an ancient city you discovered ◎ A monument honoring someone you know ◎ A new method of transportation ◎ An ad for a new candy bar, brand of sneakers, or any other product ◎ A model wearing an outfit of the future

Materials

◎ reproducible sheets (pages 53–54)
◎ crayons

Name _____ Date _____

Just Imagine...

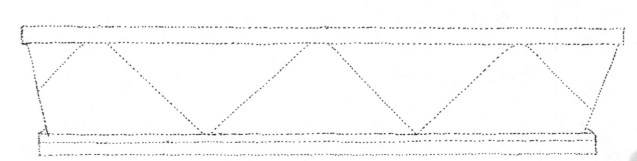

QuickArt Crayon Projects   Scholastic Professional Books

Just Imagine...

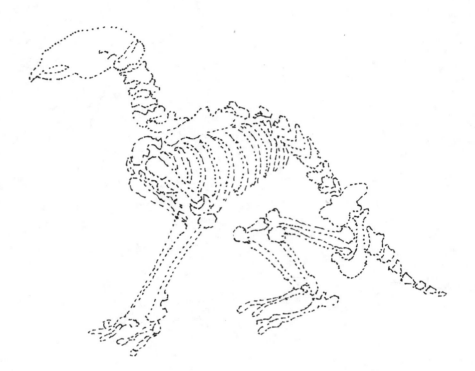

QuickArt Crayon Projects   Scholastic Professional Books

Cozy Cottage Story Starter

Launch a tale with a stand-up cottage.

This activity encourages students to use their imagination as both artists and writers. Creating a stand-up cottage will help them come up with ideas for a creative story to write on the inside.

What to Do

Have students follow these steps to make their cottages:

1 Cut out the pattern of the cottage along the dark line.

2 Fold a sheet of manila paper in half.

3 Place the left side of the pattern on the fold and the bottom of the pattern against the bottom of the manila paper.

4 In pencil, trace the outline of the top and right side of the pattern.

5 Remove the pattern and cut along the line you just drew. Be sure that you don't cut along the fold!

6 With the cottage folded shut, color the front and back with crayons or markers. Add windows, shutters, flower boxes, curtains, and so on.

7 Open the cottage and write a short story about it inside. You might give students a prompt to get started, such as:
"Once upon a time, there was a cottage in the woods. In it lived …"

8 Stand the cottages on a table or windowsill. Spread green paper underneath and have students draw roads, flowers, rivers, and so on. You can even add twigs and rocks to make it look more realistic. Invite viewers to pick up the cottages and read the stories inside.

Materials

- reproducible sheet (page 56)
- pencils
- scissors
- 8 1/2- x 11-inch sheets of manila paper
- crayons or markers

55

Cozy Cottage Story Starter

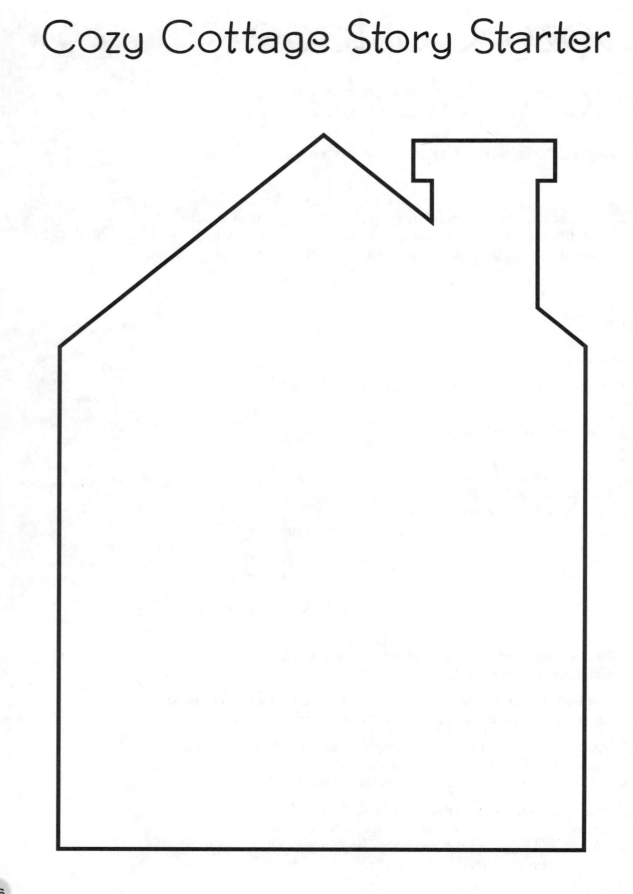

QuickArt Crayon Projects   Scholastic Professional Books

Magical Cityscape

Design a city skyline.

Your students will be delighted with their city skylines and amazed at how easy they are to draw. Just start with a few simple lines, add some details, and a city appears like magic! Demonstrate each of the steps for the class on a large sheet of newsprint. Students can do this activity individually on 8 1/2- by 11-inch paper or as a class on a large sheet of craft paper spread out on the floor or attached to a wall.

What to Do

Materials
- paper
- pencils
- crayons
- thin markers

Have students follow these steps to make their city skylines:

1 Position the paper horizontally. About one-third of the way from the bottom, draw a series of horizontal and vertical lines across the width of the paper. These are the building shapes, so use different heights and widths to make it look like an actual city skyline.

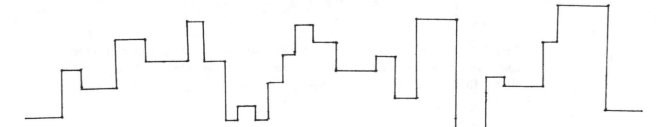

2 Add roofs, towers, spires, domes, steeples, and windows of assorted shapes.

3 Draw a second skyline not too far behind the first one. Then add roofs, windows, and other details to the new buildings.

4 When students have finished their pencil drawings, they can add color with crayons and outline the buildings in marker.

Bonus Activity

Ask your students to design a skyline of a city in the future, a city in outer space, or a lost city underwater. They can use the same technique described above. Invite children to name their cities and use the name to launch a story.

The Real Me!

Draw and compare two self-portraits.

We all think that we know what we look like ... but this activity shows students that they may need to take a second look! After students draw two self-portraits, one using a mirror and one without, they will be amazed at the differences between the two portraits. If they haven't believed it yet, this activity will prove that seeing shapes and lines is the key to drawing well.

Portrait by Joseph Merced

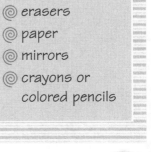

What to Do

1 Ask your students to draw a self-portrait without using a mirror.

2 Pass out mirrors for students to use while they draw and color a second self-portrait. Emphasize the importance of looking carefully at the shapes of their features. Remind them to draw the shapes that they see, not the shapes they think are there. Encourage them to think about the placement of their features in relation to each other. Here are some helpful hints and suggestions you can give students:

◎ What shape is your face? Is it long? Is it round? What shape is your chin?

◎ Note that your eyes are about halfway between the top and bottom of your head. They are not in the middle of your forehead!

◎ How close together are your eyes? Look carefully at the shape of them.

◎ How close is your mouth to your nose? How much wider is your mouth than your nose?

◎ Where do your ears appear in relation to your eyes, mouth, and nose?

◎ What shape are your eyebrows and how close are they to your eyes?

◎ Where does your hairline start? (It's about a third of the way down from the top of your head to your eyes.)

◎ Notice that your neck is thick enough to support your head.

◎ What other special features do you have? Freckles? Dimples? Bangs? Curls?

Materials
◎ pencils
◎ erasers
◎ paper
◎ mirrors
◎ crayons or colored pencils

3 Distribute crayons so that students can color their self-portraits. They may want to use several colors to match the color of their hair and skin. Demonstrate how they can overlap colors to create a new shade.

4 When they're finished, ask students to sign the backs of their drawings. Collect the pairs of portraits and hang them up together. Students will have fun noting the differences between the two portraits, and they will enjoy recognizing their classmates!

Keep Going ...

When all the portraits are displayed, have students tally and graph hair color and eye color.

Fabulous Frames

Create decorative frames for student masterpieces.

Framing a piece of artwork is the icing on the cake. It enhances the art and makes children feel even prouder of their work. First, show students how it's done. You may want to keep the framing supplies accessible so that they can make frames on their own. Making frames is also a great class project if you are planning a gala art show. More complex pieces only need plain frames, but simple pieces, like silhouettes, are enhanced by ornate settings.

What to Do

To make a simple frame:

1 Fold a piece of construction paper in half and cut out a window, leaving a border frame of one to two inches.

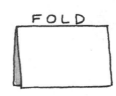

2 To make the frame more dramatic, snip or scallop interior or exterior borders.

3 For fancy frames, glue on ribbon, buttons, or cut-up lace doilies.

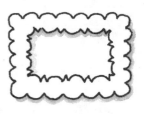

Materials

- construction paper
- scissors, tape, glue
- assorted craft supplies (buttons, ribbons, and scraps of lace or cut-up doilies)
- stencils or ordinary objects to trace
- small pieces of cardboard
- hole punches

To make a dimensional frame:

1 Clip the corners of the frame, bend the edges up as shown, and tape them in place on the back.

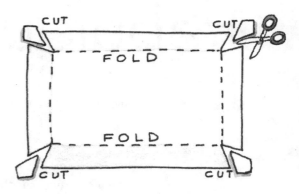

2 Leave plain or decorate as above.

3 Attach drawings to the back of the frame, using glue or tape.

To make a hanger for the frame:

1 Punch a hole on one side of a small cardboard rectangle, and fold the cardboard in half.

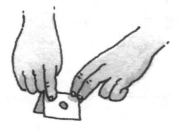

2 Use tape to attach the part without the hole to the back of the frame.

Celebrate Art!

Plan a gala student art exhibition.

After trying their artists' hands at all kinds of abstracts, contour drawings, tessellations, silhouettes, gridding, and portraiture, your students are no longer asking themselves, "What should I draw?" Now they have a wonderful new dilemma: "What do I want to draw next?" That's a giant step that deserves a celebration!

Plan an art gallery "opening." If your students have been particularly productive, the classroom probably won't be big enough to show their work and it may need to spill into the hall. Here are some ideas for the event:

What to Do

1 Set a date for the opening and send out invitations to other classes and even to parents and siblings. You can make the invitations as a class art project. First, make a plain basic invitation with the event title, date, time, and place. Then photocopy as many as you need and have students decorate them. Students can choose a theme for decorating them, such as Funny Fingerprints on page 35 or Double Doodles on page 10.

2 Start preparations. Discuss the art categories that will be included in the exhibit (abstracts, silhouettes, batik, portraits, still life, and so on). Then have the children help sort the artwork.

3 Use construction paper to mat the drawings.

4 Fasten the drawings to the gallery walls as close to children's eye level as you can. Arrange each group differently: in staggered rows, in fanned out arrangements, or even in vertical groups (but not too high).

5 Ask students to make titles for each section and for their individual drawings. If you have a classroom computer and printer, you could create museum-style labels with the name of the work, followed by the medium (such as crayon, pencil, markers, or mixed media), the artist's name, and the month and year the drawing was made. You may want to have the artists write one or two sentences about each piece, explaining what it is, how they did it, what it means, or anything else that might engage the viewers.

6 Set aside a table or long stretch of windowsill to display art books.

7 Explain to students that as artists, they should talk to the visitors about the artwork and answer any questions they might have.

8 You may want to assign students different roles to make the event run smoothly. For example, some students might greet visitors at the door, some could serve refreshments, and others could serve as guides for the exhibit. (If there aren't enough jobs for everyone, students can rotate.)

9 Plan refreshments and select background music for the event.

Enjoy the Gala!

Books About Art and Artists

A is for Artist: A Getty Museum Alphabet by J. Paul Getty (J. Paul Getty Trust Publications, 1997)

The Blue Rider: The Yellow Cow Sees the World in Blue by Doris Kutschbach (The Neues Publishing Company, 1997)

Dinosaurs, A Drawing Book by Michael Emberly (Little, Brown, 1980)

Draw 50 Animals by Lee J. Ames (Main Street Books, 1974)

The Drawing Book by Leon Baxter (Forest House, 1990)

Exploring Art Masterpieces With Young Learners by Rhonda Graff Silver (Scholastic, 1996)

Famous Artist Series (Barron's, 1994)

I Can Draw Animals by Tony Tallarico (Little Simon, 1984)

Kids' Art by Annie Harwood (Price Stern Sloan, 1995)

Talking With Artists by Pat Cummings (Simon & Schuster, 1995)

What Shall I Draw? by Ray Gibson (Usborne, 1994)

You Can Draw Amazing Faces by Kim Gamble (Dorling Kindersley Publishers, 1997)